#OFFENSIVE

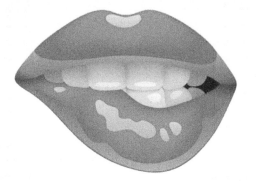

The indispensable guide to writing, delivering, and landing filthy jokes

MAD COMEDY

There are dirty jokes, and then there are jokes so depraved, so awful, so disturbed that even the raunchiest comic wouldn't dare tell them.

These are those jokes.

These are the filthiest jokes ever told.

This book is full of jokes that use the most taboo subjects – disgusting bodily functions, illicit sex, shocking religious humor, revolting acts with animals -- to make the reader simultaneously laugh and cringe.

But this book goes beyond sharing jokes so filthy that no reputable person would be caught reading it. The book teaches you to write, deliver, and land a truly vulgar joke of your own.

But first, the greatest collection of filthy, perverse, and wildly #offensive jokes ever assembled!

Little Red Riding Hood

Little Red Riding Hood is walking through the forest on the way to her grandmother's house and sees a wolf hunched under a tree with its ears erect and its mouth stretched in a big grimace.

She says to the wolf, "My, what big ears you have!"

The wolf keeps grimacing.

She says, "My, what big eyes you have!"

The wolf grimaces even wider, baring his teeth.

She says, "My, what big teeth you have!"

The wolf finally snaps and says, "Fuck off, little girl! Can't you see I'm trying to take a dump?"

Where is the safest place to fuck a hooker in New Orleans?

In the stab wound, obviously.

The Newborn Baby

John's wife was about to give birth to his first child. John was equally terrified and excited, a total nervous wreck. On the day his wife went to the hospital, John went to work but was prepared to leave as soon as he got the call that his wife was in labor.

John could barely concentrate. His mind was swimming with doubt and elation. He never had a good relationship with his own father, and he was determined not to repeat his father's sins. He'd painted the nursery, assembled the crib, installed the car seat, and studied parenting books. He'd done everything he could think of to prepare, but he was still so nervous.

As the day wore on, his doubts began to fade into unbridled anticipation. He passed cigars around the break room, and happily accepted congratulations from his coworkers. Their positivity only amplified John's joy.

Finally the call came, and John rushed from the factory, stopping only in the hospital gift shop for a huge bouquet of flowers for his wife and a teddy bear for his new pride and joy.

When he arrived at the delivery room, the doctor informed him that minor complications had forced them to do a C-section. John had to wait outside the operating room. Although it wasn't a long wait, it seemed infinite to the impatient new father. He paced up and down the busy hallway, his mind racing, thinking back to all the ways his father failed, and swearing to himself that his son would never have to experience that pain. He began to sweat profusely, and opened a hallway window for some fresh air.

'I'll never touch another drop of alcohol!' he thought. 'And I'll do with him everything I never got to do. I'll teach him baseball! I'll teach him about girls!' With every thought and future plan, his heart swelled with love.

Finally, the doctor emerged from the operating room gently carrying a tiny figure wrapped tightly in hospital blankets.

"Here's your baby boy!" the doctor announced.

John began to cry happy tears. "Oh my God! Can I hold him? Please let me hold him!"

"Of course!" said the doctor.

But as the doctor approached John, he stumbled, causing the baby to slip from his arms and hit the floor with a sickening 'thunk.'

John's scream could be heard echoing off the walls of the hospital. Nurses froze in midstep.

"Oh my God, I'm so sorry!" said the doctor, and he lunged forward to scoop the newborn off the floor. But when he bent over, he lost his balance and pitched forward with the child in his arms.

"Whoa-whoa-WHOAAAH!" The doctor stumbled across the hall and slammed into the wall.

The baby flew from his arms again and fell out of the window John opened, plummeting five stories down before landing with a splat on the roof of a parked ambulance below.

John fell to his knees with a sobbing wail, "What have you done!?!? My God, WHAT HAVE YOU DONE!!!???"

The doctor turned and said, "Nah, I'm just fucking with you, man. He was already dead."

Why did the sperm cross the road?

Because I put on the wrong sock this morning.

Dear Fuhrer

As everyone knows, Adolf Hitler absolutely adored Jews. He loved everything about the Jews: their culture, their appearance, their language, their history, everything. Once he became Fuhrer, he collected them up from all over Europe so he could pamper and protect them and lavish them with love. He even built a set of camps for his Jews to keep them safe from the war.

One morning after reviewing some troubling report on the progress of the war, Hitler finished his breakfast and decided to check on his camps. It always gave him great solace in times of trouble to meet with his Jews. He dried his little mustache and headed straight to Auschwitz to check on all his favorite Jews that he gathered there for safe keeping. Upon entering, he noticed that none of his precious Jews were anywhere to be found.

Hitler decided that they were probably finishing up in their morning shower and went to check on them. He was excited to see if they were enjoying the new floral soaps he'd sent them. After giving a few courteous knocks on the door with no response, he decided it was safe to invade their privacy just to make sure they were doing well.

But as Hitler entered the private showers, he was shocked to discover the bodies of over a thousand dead Jews piled up naked on the floor.

Hitler shrieked and ran straight to the camp commandant to ask him what the hell happened.

The commandant, confused, sputtered to Hitler, "But Mein Fuhrer! You ordered the execution of the Jews this morning right before breakfast!"

Hitler was sickened and shocked, and desperately tried to recall what he'd said before breakfast. It suddenly dawned on him.

With angry tears in his eyes, the furious Fuhrer grabbed the commandant by the lapels and shouted, "You stupid bastard! I said '*glass of juice*' not '*gas the Jews*'!"

What's red and crawls up your leg?

A homesick abortion.

The Model Employee

A man gets a new job. On his first day, his boss gives him the basic description of his duties, and he says, "No problem, boss. I know just what to do."

And sure enough, he does. The boss is amazed to see that he intuitively knows every process, where everything goes, how everything works, what everyone does.

Every day that week, the man comes in and is incredibly productive. The boss is extremely pleased.

But on Friday, the phone rings.

"Boss," says the man, "I'm sorry to say I can't come in today. I'm sick."

The boss replies, "Well, it happens. Go ahead and take the day and we'll charge it against your future sick leave."

The next week is more of the same, the man works like a maniac every day. The boss gives him more and more responsibilities, which he handles with no issues at all. Profits increase that week, which the boss attributes to the man's incredible energy and productivity.

But on Friday, the phone rings.

"Boss," says the man, "I'm sorry to say I can't come in today. I'm sick."

Now the boss is a bit taken aback. But remembering what an amazing employee the man is, he says, "OK, go ahead and take the day, and we'll charge it against your future sick leave."

The third week is the same. The man has become the boss's number one employee and right-hand man. No problem is too difficult, the boss is starting to think that maybe he can retire and let the man run the business.

But on Friday, the phone rings.

"Boss," says the man, "I'm sorry to say I can't come in today. I'm sick."

"Now just a second," says the boss. "You are the most amazing employee I've ever had. But I can't let you keep calling in sick every Friday. Is there a problem? What's going on?"

"Well," says the man, "you see, my sister was in a terrible accident and now she's paralyzed from the neck down. On Fridays I go to visit her, and she cries and cries and I console her, and one thing leads to another, and we end up fucking all day."

The boss is shocked. "What? With your sister? That's... that's disgusting!"

"I know," says the man sadly. "I keep telling you: I'm sick."

Why don't pedophiles compete in races?

They always come in a little behind.

Cream Filling

A teacher is having sex with one of her underage students in a cheap motel room. When they're done, she throws the boy's condom out the window.

As they're leaving to head back to middle school, she spots a little girl outside their motel room window holding the condom. The teacher knows she could get in real trouble if she's caught having sex with the boy.

"Hey, kid," he says to the girl, "I'll give you $20 for that."

So the girl gives it to her and takes the $20 bill. The teacher takes the condom and disposes of the evidence.

The girl runs home with $20.

"Mommy, Mommy! I got $20! A woman gave it to me for a twinky, but the jokes on her: I sucked all the cream out first!"

What do a pork pie and going down on an old woman have in common?

You have to bite through the crust and lick out the jelly before you get to the meaty bit.

The Neckbeard Incel

There once was a neckbeard incel who, despite considering himself especially chivalrous, never had any luck with the ladies. His mother, with whom he lived, thought that he needed to get laid. But the poor guy lacked any social skills, so for his thirty-first birthday, she bought him a prostitute for the night.

When he gets in bed with her, the hooker asks him what he would like to do. He doesn't know, so she starts listing off positions and other miscellaneous sex acts.

"How about 69?" she asks.

Blushing, but not knowing what it is, he chooses 69, so she gets on top and they go at it.

Now, the prostitute had some bad food earlier in the day, and her stomach is a little upset. She can't help it: she lets out a little fart. Thinking he wouldn't notice, she continues. But the pressure is terrible, and she farts a second time.

Feeling a little guilty, she asks the man how he's doing.

He lifts his head between her legs and says, "I'm doing okay, but I don't know if I can take 67 more of those!"

What do bungee jumping and sex with your sister have in common?

If the rubber breaks, you're dead.

The New iPhone

I just had the most uncomfortable experience of my life.

I've always wanted an iPhone but never had one before, so I go to the Apple Store to have a look. So there I am, when this middle aged guy comes up next to me, like really close. And then he starts asking me if I like the new iPhone, what do I think about the camera, am I thinking of getting one, etc, and I'm like "Yeah, it's pretty good."

I'm trying to play it cool because I don't wanna admit that there's no way I could even afford one if I wanted to. I mean, I'm only 17, and don't have a job or anything. But then after a while, his comments start becoming personal, first complimenting my shoes and calling me a 'strapping young lad'.

Now I'm quite weirded out but figured he's just new at sales and really bad at it. But after a while I realized he's not a staff member, that he doesn't work there. So now I'm fully freaked out. This guy just came up to me and all up in my personal space, so I try to ignore him (but not trying to be subtle about it). I turn away, and get this, he sort of grabs my arm to turn me back and gives it a little squeeze and says something along the lines of, "Oh, you've been hitting the gym, yeah?"

I turn to look at him and say, "Excuse me, do not touch me," and quickly leave the Apple Store.

This guy follows me out and catches up to me, all apologetic, saying how sorry he is and he didn't realize he was annoying me and all that.

And as I'm about to say "Yeah, okay, fine, whatever", he says "Listen, here's the thing. If you give me a blowjob, I will give you this new iPhone XS" and pulls out this new iPhone, fresh in the box.

I was flabbergasted. I genuinely thought I'd misheard him, so had to clarify and said "What? You want me to suck you off for a phone? Really?!"

And he smiled and nodded.

Some people are fucking disgusting. Makes me sick.

Sent from my iPhone

Why don't men go down on women first thing in the morning?

Have you ever tried to pull apart a cold grilled cheese sandwich?

The Bet Jar

A dirty homeless man walks into a bar and sees an enormous jar filled with a mountain of $5 bills. He asks the bartender what the jar is for.

"It's our bet jar. Been collecting money for almost six years now."

"Wow," says the homeless man, "I've never seen that much cash."

"Tell you what," the bartender says, "Why don't you try it? You put $5 in the jar, and I'll give you three tasks. If you finish them, you'll get the jar filled with money."

The man says "What? All of it? I'll play!"

He puts his last $5 in the jar.

The bartender smiles and tells him, "The first task is drinking this handle of tequila without stopping, crying, or flinching. The second task is to go out back and pull the rotted tooth out of my Doberman. And the third and final task is to go upstairs and give my poor old grandma one last wild night of exotic pleasure sex."

The homeless man grabs the bottle of tequila and chugs it. Sweat pours down his red face, but he doesn't flinch or cry. But when he finishes, it's obvious he's drunk out of his mind. He practically falls off his bar stool and stumbles outside to the dog.

From inside the bar, all the patrons heard growling and snarling and barking and then a dog whimpering until finally the man comes back inside the bar.

Bloodied and battered with his clothes ripped to shreds and reeking of tequila, he slurs, "All right, where's the lady with the bad tooth?"

A man walks into his daughter's room and catches her masturbating furiously with a cucumber.

Her angry dad yells at her, "What the hell are you doing? Now it's going to taste like salad!"

The Queen of England

The Queen of England and a famous porn star died on the same day. Both of them made it up to the Pearly Gates at the same time, but when they fronted up to Saint Peter, he told them there was only one space left for that day. They'd have to argue their respective cases.

The porn start ripped off her top and said, "These are the most perfect breasts God ever created, and I'm sure it will please him greatly to be able to gaze upon them for eternity."

Saint Peter eyed her luscious tits and smiled appreciatively.

The Queen said nothing, but hiked up her skirt, pulled down her undies, shook up a bottle of Perrier she had in her handbag, then started to douche her twat with it.

Even the porn star was horrified at the sight of a wrinkly old monarch in her 90s sticking a bottle in her dusty old hooch.

But Saint Peter just nodded and let the Queen pass through the pearly gates.

"What the fuck is all that about?" yelled the porn star. "I show you two of God's greatest achievements and NOTHING! That old bitch performs an absolutely revolting act and you let her in?"

"Sorry, love," said Saint Peter, "but a royal flush beats a pair every time."

What's the difference between sand and afterbirth?

You can't gargle with sand.

Gay Marriage

Two gay men, Paul and Tom, were recently married and couldn't keep their hands off one another. They were making love one night and had just finished when Paul decided he was going to freshen up in the shower.

Tom was laying there thinking about how wonderful Paul was, and he decided he was going to join him in the shower.

When Tom got into the bathroom, he opened the shower curtain and the first thing he saw was a large cumshot on the wall.

He wailed to Tom, "I can't believe you! We just finished making love, and you come in here and jack off?"

Paul looks at the wall and says "What are you talking about? I wasn't jacking off -- I farted!"

How do you get a dog to quit humping your leg?

Pick him up and suck his dick.

The Poultry Solution

A man has just been released from prison after serving seven long years behind bars and finds himself feeling really, really, really horny. He's also short on money. Nevertheless, he heads to his local bordello in search of some relief.

He walks in, goes to the nice lady at the front desk, and slaps a $5 bill on the counter.

"Lady, this is all the money I got, but I really need some satisfaction, if you get my meaning. What can you do for me?"

The nice lady eyes him, collects the money from the counter, and says, "Well, we don't usually do this, but if you go down the hall, third door on your RIGHT, you should find what you need."

The man thanks her, then makes his way down the hall to the third door on the right and goes in. In the middle of room on the floor is a mattress, and on that mattress is a chicken.

At first, the man is grossed out. A chicken?!? But it's been seven years. His urges get the best of him and he ends up having sex with the chicken. He leaves the bordello with a smile on his face, surprised at how much he enjoyed himself.

The next day, the man finds himself really horny again, but with even less money. Still, he heads back to the bordello hoping to get lucky again. He walks in, goes to the nice lady at the front desk, and puts three wrinkly dollar bills on the counter.

"Lady, this is all the money I got, but I really need some satisfaction, if you get my meaning. What can you do for me?"

The nice lady sighs and collects the money, "You again, huh? Go down the hall, third door on your LEFT this time, you'll find what you need."

The man thanks her, then makes his way down the hall to the third door on the left, and goes in.

This room is set up as a theater, and there are several men jerking off to a video playing of a man having sex with an inflatable doll.

Our hero sees this and exclaims in disgust, "This is terrible. I can't get off on this. This is some depraved shit."

One of other patrons hears him and says, "Aww, this is nothin'. Yesterday, we seen some guy fuckin' a chicken!"

What's the difference between hungry and horny?

Where you stick the cucumber.

The Fisherman

A man was fishing off the dock along a picturesque lake by a romantic hotel in the country, when another man came and sat down. By way of conversation, the man asked the other what he was doing there.

"I'm on my honeymoon," the fisherman said.

"Oh. Shouldn't you be having sex with your wife?"

"Well, I would be. But she has a yeast infection."

"What about oral sex?"

"Canker sores."

"Anal sex?"

"Diarrhea."

The man paused, thinking, while the other man reeled in his line.

"Pardon my question, but why are you here with her?"

"Well, I like fishing. And she's got worms."

What's the worst part about going down on your grandmother?

Banging your head on the lid of the coffin.

The Cowboy

A cowboy rides his horse up to a saloon. He dismounts and ties the reins to a hitching post outside the saloon. Before he walks in, he stops, lifts his horse's tail, and kisses his horse right on the butthole.

All the patrons in the saloon gawk.

The cowboy saunters into the saloon, takes off his hat, and steps up the bar.

"Whiskey," he orders.

The entire saloon is silent.

The stunned bartender serves him and then asks, "Mind if I ask why'd ya kiss your horse on the butt?"

The cowboy grunts, "It's 'cuz I got chapped lips."

The bartender asks, "And does horse manure help them heal?"

The cowboy tosses back his whiskey and replies, "No, but it keeps me from lickin' 'em."

What do you get when you turn a blonde upside down?

A brunette with bad breath.

The Bus Rider

I was on the bus the other day when this attractive young woman started to breastfeed her child. An elderly woman got up and protested, saying it was the most disgusting thing she'd ever seen, and she would complain to the bus company.

In hindsight, I really shouldn't have been jerking off at the time.

What's the difference between jam and jelly?

I can't jelly my dick up your ass.

The Burger

A man sits at the counter in a diner and orders a hamburger.

The huge guy behind the counter bellows, "One burger!"

Whereupon the chef grabs a huge hunk of chopped meat, stuffs it in his bare armpit, pumps his arm a few times to squeeze it flat, and then tosses it on the grill.

Nearly falling off his stool, the man says, "That's the most disgusting thing I've ever seen!"

"Yeah?" says the guy behind the counter. "You should be here in the morning when he makes the doughnuts."

What do a nearsighted gynecologist and a puppy have in common?

A wet nose.

The Pet Rabbit

A guy finds his dog with the neighbor's pet rabbit in its mouth. The rabbit is dead and the guy panics. He knows the rabbit belongs to his neighbor's daughter, and she'll be despondent. He also knows that he's been warned repeatedly to keep his dog in his own yard. If he gets caught with his dog running loose again, his landlord will kick him out.

So he takes the dirty, chewed up rabbit into his house. He gives the dead rabbit a bath, gently soaping away the blood, and then took a blow dryer to dry and fluff its fur.

Then he sneaks over to his neighbor's house and quietly puts it back into the cage in their backyard, hoping they will think it died of natural causes.

A few days later, the neighbor asks the guy, "Did you hear that Fluffy died?"

The guy stammers and says, "Um... no... what happened?"

The neighbor replies, "We found him dead in his cage one day. But the weird thing is that the day after we buried him, someone dug him up, gave him a bath and put him back into the cage. There are some really sick people out there!"

What did Cinderella do when she got to the ball?

She gagged.

Infidelity

A young man came home one night and told his father, "Dad, I fell in love and want to date this awesome girl!"

His father turned off the TV and leaned forward in his recliner and said with a smile, "That's great, son! Who is she?"

"It's Sandra, the neighbor's daughter."

His father slumped back in his chair and said, "Ohhh, I wish you hadn't said that! I have to tell you something, son, but you must promise not to tell your mother. Sandra is actually your sister."

The boy is naturally bummed out, but a couple of months later, he walks in with a big grin.

"Dad, I fell in love again and she is even hotter!"

His father smiled with relief and said, "That's great, son! Who is she?"

"It's Angela, the other neighbor's daughter."

His father shook his head sadly, "Ohhh, I wish you hadn't said that. Angela is also your sister."

This went on a few more times. With every girl, he got madder and madder at his father. Finally, he went to his mother and told her everything about his father's infidelity.

"Mom, I am so mad at dad! I've fallen in love with six girls, but I can't date any of them because dad is the father of all of them!"

The mother hugs him affectionately and says, "You can date whoever you want, darling. He isn't *your* father!"

What's the definition of 'disgusting'?

Sticking eight oysters up your grandma's vagina -- and sucking out nine.

The Frisbee

A woman is washing dishes when she sees a group of young boys standing around the trunk of the big tree in her backyard. They've all got their phones out and the cameras are aimed up the tree. The woman goes out to investigate and spots her 13-year-old daughter wearing her nicest skirt and a cute top way up the tree. The boys scatter.

"Sarah? Honey, what are you doing up that tree?"

"The boys got their frisbee stuck up here again. They keep asking me to go get it."

"Oh, sweetheart, those naughty boys just want to get a peek at your underwear!"

The pretty little girl climbs down, adjusts her skirt, and says, "The joke's on them, mom! I'm not wearing any underwear!"

Yesterday, I caught a disgusting pervert on the bus watching porn.

Over my shoulder.

The Livestock Lesson

A farmer was tending to his livestock when he noticed that one of his cows was completely cross-eyed.

He called up a veterinarian, who drove out to examine the cow. The vet took one look at the cow, stuck a tube up the cow's butt, and blew into the tube until the cow's eyes straightened out.

The vet charged the farmer a four hundred bucks for the service.

About a week later, the cow's eyes were cross-eyed again. The farmer didn't want to pay $400 again for such a simple procedure. He figured he could probably take care of it himself.

The farmer called his hired hand over, and together they put a tube up the cow's butt.

The farmer put his lips to the tube and started to blow. Strangely, nothing happened. The cow remained cross-eyed.

The hired hand said, "Here, let me try."

The farmer stepped aside. The hired hand removed the tube, turned it around, put it in the cow's butt and started to blow.

"What are you doing?" asked the farmer, horrified.

"Well, I ain't gonna use the side that you had your lips on."

How do you make your husband scream during sex?

Call him and let him hear it.

The Dentist

An old woman scheduled an appointment with a dentist. On the day of the appointment, she filled out the forms and waited patiently until she was led back to the examination room. She climbed up in the dentist's chair.

The dentist entered, and as he pulled on his gloves, he saw the old woman hike her skirt up, pull her panties off, and spread her legs wide.

The dentist, taken aback, said, "I'm sorry, ma'am, but I think you're in the wrong office."

"No, I'm not," said the woman. "You put in my husband's new teeth last week."

"And?" the stunned dentist asked.

"Now you have to remove them."

Know what old pussy tastes like?

Depends.

The Anti-Vaxxer

A woman penned a thoughtful and well-researched article that was published in a major newspaper that clearly articulated why vaccines are an unnatural evil that instead of preventing disease actually *cause* mental and physical disease instead.

The woman closed her article with a line straight from the heart, "That's why I'm the proud anti-vaxx mother of five beautiful children."

Shortly after the article was published, the newspaper was forced to issue several corrections:

Correction 1: four beautiful children

Correction 2: three beautiful children

Correction 3: two beautiful children

What's the difference between a lentil and a chickpea?

I've never had a lentil on my chest.

The Good Doctor

An old doctor had sex with one of his patients and felt guilty all day long. No matter how much he tried to forget about it, he just couldn't. The guilt was overwhelming.

But, every once in a while, he would hear a reassuring voice in his head that said, "Don't worry about it. You aren't the first medical practitioner to have sex with one of his patients and you won't be the last. Just let it go."

But invariably another voice in his head would bring him back to reality, whispering: "You're a veterinarian, you sick bastard!"

No one likes to watch disgusting and degrading pornography...

More than I do.

Sweet Little Kindergarteners

On the last day of kindergarten, all the children brought presents for their teacher.

The florist's son handed the teacher a gift.

She shook it, held it up and said, "I bet I know what it is - it's some flowers!"

"That's right!" shouted the little boy.

Then the candy store owner's daughter handed the teacher a gift.

She held it up, shook it and said. "I bet I know what it is - it's a box of candy!"

"That's right!" shouted the little girl.

The next gift was from the liquor store owner's son. The teacher held it up and saw that it was leaking. She touched a drop with her finger and tasted it.

"Is it wine?" she asked.

"No," the little boy answered.

The teacher touched another drop to her tongue.

"Is it champagne?" she asked.

"No," he answered.

Finally, the teacher said, "I give up. What is it?"

The little boy proudly replied, "A puppy!"

Did you hear about the poor single mom who found a back-alley doctor to perform a cheap circumcision for her son?

It was a rip off.

The Proctologist

A proctologist was a well-known specialist treating homosexuals who, because of their fondness for anal sex, often have specific issues with the anus, rectum, and colon.

One patient calls the office requesting an appointment. The nurse asks him about his condition, and the caller explains that he keeps shitting lettuce.

"Shitting... *lettuce?*" the nurse asks.

"Yes, shitting lettuce," he confirms.

She schedules him for an appointment that day. The doctor has him undress and bend over the examining room table. The doctor takes a look and, sure enough, there's a piece of lettuce sticking out the patient's asshole.

The doctor has seen a lot of terrible conditions over the years, but he's so disgusted by this sight, he can't help telling the patient how disgusting it is.

The patient shakes his head and replies, "Doc, that's just the tip of the iceberg."

Three women are sitting at a bar arguing over who has the biggest vagina.

The first girl says, "My boyfriend can fit a whole fist up there."

The second girl says, "Ha, my boyfriend can fit two fists and a foot."

The third girl just smiles as she slides down the bar stool.

The Movie Score

A pianist was hired to play background music for a movie. He was so excited to get such an important job. For years, he'd been making ends meet by teaching piano lessons to kids, but now he was finally achieving his lifelong dream. He was a professional musician! He poured his heart and soul into the work, and he was very pleased with the end result. He listened to the recording over and over, and was certain he'd done it flawlessly. When it was completed, he asked when and where he could see the movie.

The producer sheepishly confessed that it was actually a pornographic film and it was due out in a month.

A month later, the musician reluctantly went to a porn theatre to see the adult movie.

With his collar up and dark glasses on, he took a seat in the back row of the adult cinema, next to a couple who also seemed to be in disguise.

The movie was even raunchier than he had feared, featuring group sex, bondage, and even an especially raunchy scene involving a dog. All the while, his musical accompaniment was playing.

After a while watching the adult movie, the embarrassed pianist turned to the couple and said, "I'm only here to listen to the music."

"Yeah?" replied the man. "We're only here to see our dog."

Why doesn't Santa Claus have any children?

Because he only comes once a year and it's down your chimney.

Old Timers

Bill and John, both men in their 80s and in failing health, decided that because they weren't going to live much longer, they'd sneak out of their nursing home together to visit a whorehouse one last time.

The Madam of the whorehouse knew the two old men very well. She hadn't seen them in years, but they were notorious for roughing up the girls. When the Madam heard that Bill and John had arrived, she decided to take advantage of the two old bastards. She quickly prepared two blow-up dolls, placing one in each room on the bed. She then went down to greet the old men.

Bill and John greeted her like an old friend before telling her, "We are here for the last time".

The Madam told them she'd take care of everything, but prices had gone up. They each had to pay $5,000. The men looked at each other, shrugged, and paid her with money that should have gone to their family inheritance.

The Madam sent Bill upstairs to the room on the left and John to the room on the right.

After an hour Bill and John left the rooms, met each other in the hallway without a word, and left together. They walked back to the nursing home together.

Bill and John were very quiet until Bill said, "How was yours?"

John said quietly, "I think she was dead. How was yours?"

Bill said, "I think she was a witch."

John replied, "A witch? How do you know she was a witch?"

Bill said, "Well, I climbed on top of her just like in the old days, but when I bit her nipple, she farted and flew out the window."

Did you hear about the constipated mathematician?

He worked it out with a pencil.

The Toothbrush Salesman

Three guys begin work at a toothbrush company as salesmen.

Each day, two of the guys sell twenty toothbrushes, but the third guy, Dave, consistently sells five hundred toothbrushes.

The other two guys are jealous, but they can't figure out his secret. They're selling the same toothbrushes at the same prices. They got the same training. They can't understand how he's doing it.

Then, one day, they run into him at the mall, where he's set up a table offering free chocolate samples.

"This is your secret?" says the first guy dubiously.

"Yep. Try some chocolate," says Dave.

They both take a little bit of chocolate and put it in their mouths.

"Eww!" says the first guy.

"This tastes like shit!" says the second guy.

"It is shit," Dave nods, "Would you like to buy a toothbrush?"

Why did Jesus die on the cross?

He forgot the safeword.

The Helpful Stranger

Bob walks into a public bathroom and notices a guy with no arms standing next to a urinal. As Bob takes care of his business, he wonders how the poor soul is going to take a leak. Bob finishes and heads for the door, but then stops because he figures he should ask the man if he needs help.

"Oh yes, please," the man cries. "You have a kind heart, sir," says the man with no arms.

But as Bob unzips the man and pulls his willy out, he encounters all kinds of mold, red bumps, moles, scabs, scars, and other unpleasant-looking things.

The armless man asks Bob to kindly point it at the urinal and then shake it, put it back, and zip it.

So Bob gathers his courage, shuts his eyes and does so.

"Thank you very much, sir!" says the armless man.

"No problem," says Bob, "but what the hell is wrong with your penis?"

The guy pulls his arms out of his shirt and says, "I don't know, but I ain't touching it!"

A man asks the woman standing in line next to him,
"Can I smell your feet?"

"No!" she replies indignantly.

He replies, "Oh, then it must be your pussy!"

The Jumper

A beautiful young woman is standing on the side of a bridge, trembling and crying with her makeup streaked with tears, looking over the side of the bridge at the road far below. It's obvious she's thinking about jumping off to her death.

A homeless drunk spots her as he walks by, and starts to stumble toward her.

The lady notices the man coming and says, tearfully, "Go away! There's nothing you can say to me to change my mind. You cannot help me."

"Hey, look, pretty lady," he slurs, "if you're going to kill yourself anyway, do you mind if I screw you first?"

"What? You disgusting pig! Can't you see I'm distraught? Go away!"

The homeless man turns and starts walking away.

The lady calls after him, "Is that all you're going to say to me? Nothing more? Won't you try to convince me that life is worth living that I shouldn't jump? Where's your humanity? Where are you going?"

The homeless man calls back to her, "I have to get down below the bridge. If I hurry, you'll still be warm."

What did one gay sperm say to the other gay sperm?

How are we supposed to find an egg in all this shit?

The Farming Lesson

A small farming family live on a picturesque farm far from town. There's a red barn, a pretty white farmhouse, and green fields with rows of crops popping up.

The farmer is sitting in the kitchen one morning when his son comes in from the barn with a large glass of white liquid.

He is so excited because he's just milked his first cow.

The boy then takes a big drink from the glass.

The farmer just stares at his son.

After the boy finishes his glass, the farmer says, "Son, there are a few things you need to learn about farming. First and foremost – and this is important -- we don't have a cow. We have a bull."

Why do farts smell?

So deaf people can enjoy them, too.

An Evening at the Movies

Two old ladies, lifelong friends, decide to go to the movies together. They slowly drive to the theater, wait in line for tickets, buy some popcorn even though it gets stuck in their dentures, and make their way to the theater. They choose seats next to each other in the middle of the theater, not too close to the screen, and not too far.

After a while, the theater fills up, the lights dim, and the movie starts.

After about a half hour, one old lady whispers to the other, "Psst!"

"What?" she whispers back.

"I think the young man next to me is… masturbating!"

"What makes you say that?"

"He's using my hand."

What's the ultimate rejection?

When you're masturbating and your hand falls asleep.

The Birthday Party

At my son's birthday party, I tried to get along with my girlfriend's parents, but they've never liked me. Right in front of everyone, they called me a disgusting creep just because I'm 38 and she's 24.

They really ruined our son's 10th birthday party.

What's the difference between a needy, clingy, whiny woman and a light bulb?

You can unscrew a light bulb.

The Expensive Girl

A young man has only been working as a stock broker for a few weeks before he suddenly landed a major deal. It was the kind of multi-million dollar deal that other traders work for years to land, and he pulled it off in just weeks. He was awarded an enormous bonus and a promotion.

Now, the young man had been working tirelessly, day and night, since he started his job, and hadn't had time for a relationship. He decided to reward himself by renting a high-end call girl for the night. He found a girl online who looked like a model: a tall, long-legged, sultry exotic beauty. He happily paid the $10,000 fee for one night of pleasure with the amazing girl.

When he meets her, he's astonished at her beauty. It's been months since he's had sex, so he immediately takes her back to his apartment. He practically drags he into the bedroom and goes down on her a bit to get things lubed up.

While he's down there, he gets something in his mouth and sits up and spits it into his hand. It's a slimy, bloody, mucus-covered slug. He shakes his head and goes back down again for a minute till he feels something else in his mouth. He sits up and spits out a piece of a squirming, bloody worm.

He looks at the escort, gagged, and said, "I think I'm going to be sick!"

In the cutest French accent, she said, "That's what the last guy said, too."

How do you know that you have a high sperm count?

She has to chew before she swallows.

The Affliction

A woman settles into her seat on a plane. As she gets her pillow and mask out preparing for the long flight ahead, she hears the man sitting beside her sneeze. She looks over to say, 'Bless you', but before she can get the words out, she's startled to see the man unzipping his pants. He pulls out his penis, wipes it off, tucks it back in, and zips up his trousers.

The woman is in absolute disbelief. She starts to wonder if her mind is playing tricks on her, because there is no way that is what just happened. But then, the man sneezes again. The woman looks over, and again, the man unzips his trousers, pulls out his penis, wipes it off, tucks in back in, and zips up like nothing happened.

Now the woman knows her mind is not playing tricks on her -- and she is furious.

She looks over at the man and says, "Excuse me!"

But just then, he sneezes again, and again he unzips, pulls out, wipes off, tucks, zips, and turns to the woman and says, "Sorry, can I help you?"

The woman starts letting him have it.

"That is unacceptable! If you think for one second I am going to put up with that disgusting display this entire flight you have a..."

"Sorry ma'am," the man interrupts, "but I have a medical condition, that causes me to have an orgasm every time I sneeze."

The woman feeling a bit embarrassed that she was so judgmental, starts to feel some sympathy for the man.

"Oh! I see," she says in a sympathetic voice, "I am very sorry for my reaction, that must be a very hard condition to live with. You are very brave to live a normal life. Tell me, do you take anything for your condition?"

The man replies, "Yes, as a matter of fact I do: pepper."

Why did God create the yeast infection?

So women know what it's like to deal with an angry cunt.

The Brilliant Musician

A talented but unemployed jazz pianist and composer was walking down Second Avenue in New York contemplating his sad life when he sees a sign in a restaurant window that says, 'Jazz pianist wanted, full time position.'

Elated at his good fortune, he goes inside to apply for the job.

He meets the manager, who takes him to the corner of the restaurant where there is a freshly tuned, gleaming black Steinway grand piano. The pianist is momentarily overcome as he sits down at the majestic instrument.

 The manager pulls up a chair and tells him that the position pays three hundred dollars a night, but with one condition: "You have to play only original music."

Barely able to contain his joy, the pianist says, "That's not a problem at all, I've written hundreds of pieces."

The manager asks him to play one.

The pianist launches into an up-tempo post-bop piece with subtly shifting harmonies somewhat reminiscent of Ravel, but with a rhythmic drive that would make McCoy Tyner blush.

After he finishes the tune, the manager, floored, asks "Wow! that's amazing! What's the name of that?"

The pianist tells him, "It's called 'I love it when you take a huge steaming shit in my grandmother's mouth'."

The manager is taken aback by the unexpected vulgarity, but because the pianist is so brilliant, he ignores it. The manager asks him to play another of his compositions. The man starts off with a poignant rubato introduction and then smoothly slides into a 5/4 samba that features a bi-tonal ostinato section set off by a funk groove section with a surprising update of Coltrane's countdown changes.

The manager is again thoroughly impressed and, with some trepidation, asks the name of the tune.

The pianist says, "It's called 'I want to stick my head in your panties and suffocate in your wonderfully sickening ass-stench.'"

The manager is again startled by the sharply disgusting title, but by this time a crowd had gathered around to enjoy the music.

Realizing that he was in the presence of greatness, the manager decides to hire him, but gives him a warning: "You must promise me one thing: you can't tell anyone the names of your tunes."

The pianist gives the manager a bemused look, and although he doesn't fully understand this strange request, he agrees.

So the pianist starts his new job and the crowd is really enjoying his other-worldly dinner music. After a while, nature makes its inevitable call, and he takes a break to go to the men's room. Never the most fastidious person, and being pre-occupied with an idea for a new composition, the pianist neglects to return his manhood to his trousers, and blithely strides out of the men's room.

Mistaking the diners' stares for adulation, he confidently struts toward the piano.

But before he gets there the bartender, shocked, yells out, "Hey man! Do you know your fly is open and your dick and balls are hanging out?"

The pianist gives him a condescending look and says, "Do I know it? I *wrote* it!"

How do you tell if a clam is a guy or girl?

Smash it against the wall. If it screams, "Agghh! My balls!" then it's a guy.

The Motorcycle

When I finished high school, I wanted to take my graduation money and buy myself a motorcycle, but my mom said no.

You see, I had a older brother who died in a horrible motorcycle accident when he was eighteen.

So she said I could just have his motorcycle.

How to Write an #Offensive Joke

Dirty jokes are certainly not new: some of the earliest recorded jokes, told thousands of years ago, deal with things that people do in the bathroom or the bedroom. What makes these jokes funny? What makes any joke funny?

Experts say that humor is based on incongruity. That is, jokes are based on surprise, on elements that don't go together.

So why are dirty jokes especially funny? Dirty jokes have a built-in incongruity: we're already talking about taboo subjects. Every one of them says things that people don't talk about in polite company. The listener automatically thinks, "I can't believe we're talking about this!" They don't fit in normal conversation, so just hearing them is incongruous.

There is an old four-word joke that demonstrates incongruity:

Battered women: sounds delicious!

Making fun of the abuse of women is no joking matter, right? The surprise use of the alternate meaning of battered makes this twist devilishly delicious. Incongruity added to taboo subjects is sure to elicit a laugh.

But the best of them combine multiple layers of expectation-disrupting incongruity – often in a single line – with a cringe-inducing violation of a societal taboo.

Take, for example, the following joke:

> *Where is the safest place to fuck a hooker in New Orleans?*

Now, obviously, this is incongruous, because the premise assumes you'd hire a prostitute in New Orleans, which is both illegal and considered shameful. It's also layered with loaded words: not just the casual use of profanity, but the inclusion of 'safest place'. Safe from what? Disease? The police? Violent pimps? Thieving prostitutes? An unhappy spouse? The joke also places the reader in New Orleans, a city famous for Mardi Gras and the accompanying wild and often lewd behavior. This joke could go in many directions. But the punchline is exploding with incongruity:

> *In the stab wound, obviously.*

Yes, the incongruity of New Orleans prostitutes having stab wounds -- and the idea of having sex in such a stab wound – violates many taboos. The head-fake in the original question of 'where' in New Orleans meaning which of the prostitute's orifices creates an unexpected incongruity. But the inclusion of the single word 'obviously' adds a whole new dimension to the joke. In a mere seventeen words, this joke delivers a full blast of surprising and cringe-worthy incongruity to the reader.

Now take the following:

> *What do bungee jumping and sex with your girlfriend have in common?*
>
> *If the rubber breaks, you're dead.*

This joke is mildly funny and slightly risqué. A man having sex with his girlfriend is, of course, commonplace. The implied danger, though, is pregnancy and the associated risks related to out-of-wedlock pregnancy, including some implied risk of violence, presumably from the father of the girlfriend.

To make it funnier, one could increase the intensity of the incongruity or the taboo nature of the joke. To increase the incongruity, instead of sex with your girlfriend, it could be with your underage girlfriend, boss's wife, neighbor's daughter, or your own sister:

> *What do bungee jumping and sex with your sister have in common?*
>
> *If the rubber breaks, you're dead.*

Or change the nature of the danger to make the implied risk more severe while at the same time violating more taboos:

> *What do bungee jumping and anal sex with a diseased transgender prostitute have in common?*
>
> *If the rubber breaks, you're dead.*

So how does it work? First of all, a joke is a story! Understand the elements of a story to understand how to construct a powerful joke.

Every story has five key elements:

- Character
- Setting
- Plot
- Conflict

- Theme

Elements of a Joke

Let's look at the joke that opened the book:

The Newborn Baby.

John's wife was about to give birth to his first child. John was equally terrified and excited, a total nervous wreck. On the day his wife went to the hospital, John went to work but was prepared to leave as soon as he got the call that his wife was in labor.

John could barely concentrate. His mind was swimming with doubt and elation. He never had a good relationship with his own father, and he was determined not to repeat his father's sins. He'd painted the nursery, assembled the crib, installed the car seat, and studied parenting books. He'd done everything he could think of to prepare, but he was still so nervous.

As the day wore on, his doubts began to fade into unbridled anticipation. He passed cigars around the break room, and happily accepted congratulations from his coworkers. Their positivity only amplified John's joy.

Finally the call came, and John rushed from the factory, stopping only in the hospital gift shop for a huge bouquet of flowers for his wife and a teddy bear for his new pride and joy.

When he arrived at the delivery room, the doctor informed him that minor complications had forced them to do a C-section. John had to wait outside the operating room. Although it wasn't a long wait, it seemed infinite to the impatient new father. He paced up and down the busy hallway, his mind racing, thinking back to all the ways his father failed, and swearing to himself that his son would never have to experience that pain. He began to sweat profusely, and opened a hallway window for some fresh air.

'I'll never touch another drop of alcohol!' he thought. 'And I'll do with him everything I never got to do. I'll teach him baseball! I'll teach him about girls!' With every thought and future plan, his heart swelled with love.

Finally, the doctor emerged from the operating room gently carrying a tiny figure wrapped tightly in hospital blankets.

"Here's your baby boy!" the doctor announced.

John began to cry happy tears. "Oh my God! Can I hold him? Please let me hold him!"

"Of course!" said the doctor.

But as the doctor approached John, he stumbled, causing the baby to slip from his arms and hit the floor with a sickening 'thunk.'

John's scream could be heard echoing off the walls of the hospital. Nurses froze in midstep.

"Oh my God, I'm so sorry!" said the doctor, and he lunged forward to scoop the newborn off the floor. But when he bent over, he lost his balance and pitched forward with the child in his arms.

"WhooooOOAAAH!" The doctor stumbled across the hall and slammed into the wall.

The baby flew from his arms again and fell out of the window John opened, plummeting five stories down before landing with a splat on the roof of a parked ambulance.

John fell to his knees with a sobbing wail, "What have you done!?!? My God, WHAT HAVE YOU DONE!!!???"

The doctor turned and said, "Nah, I'm just fucking with you, man. He was already dead."

This joke uses the audience's expectations and experiences against them. The first-time father experience is familiar: the expectation, the nervousness. That familiarity is manipulated through a long setup developing the character, John, and giving him a backstory: an unhappy childhood he doesn't wish to perpetuate upon his own child.

There's a further built-in audience expectation that is manipulated: that of the doctor as trusted and serious.

The surprise in this joke comes from the doctor intentionally using a stillborn child as a prop in a childish prank played on the father. The violation of taboo is both breaking the news of an infant's death by pranking a grieving father and the grotesque physical destruction of a newborn.

The violation of taboo and the masterful setup of incongruity make this joke a masterpiece of dark humor.

This joke has all the elements of story:

Character – In the case of this joke, the characters are a man and a doctor. We also have an antagonist and a protagonist as we'll discuss in a moment.

Setting – We're at home, then at work, and then in a hospital

Plot – The plot a man is nervous about the birth of his first son

Conflict – The baby is stillborn

Theme – Marriage and relationships.

The buildup to this joke is long and involved, and seemingly unnecessary: why go into such detail over the man's agonizing of his relationship with his father, or detail his experience handing out cigars at work?

The buildup is used so the audience sympathizes with John, and now treats him as the protagonist of the story. Jokes that have this built in, have an extra impact on the audience: emotion. Now they are not only listening to a joke, but in a subtle way they are rooting for the protagonist. They are actually yearning for (at some level) John to win.

And they're shocked into laughter at the punchline when the doctor, who they previously considered a trusted actor, is in fact the antagonist. That plot twist drives the surprise and generates the laughter.

And in storytelling that is powerful.

In that way, jokes and stories are exactly the same.

To understand how to write a joke, we must first understand why people laugh.

Laughter Triggers

Fact: The number one element that triggers human laughter is SURPRISE. It's like magic, only with words. A magician surprises the audience when he does his trick. If there is no surprise, there is no trick. The formula for any magician is to have surprise. Without formulating surprise, you're gonna have one hell of a boring act.

It's the same with comedy.

Scientists have identified two other major reasons humans laugh: embarrassment and recognition.

The key is for any joke to work is surprise (often known as the 'plot twist'), of course, but weaving in both embarrassment (including violating taboos) and recognition (by personalizing it to the audience experience or having them identify with a character, setting, plot, conflict, and/or theme) increases the hilarity.

So how do we create surprise? The easiest way to create surprise is to lead the audience to assume one thing, then surprise them with something different. (See how it's similar to magic?)

I woke up in the hotel this morning with a vicious hangover, and the housekeeper was banging on the door. The noise was killing me and she just wouldn't stop.

Finally, I had to get up and let her out.

Let's look at the joke. It's a common situation. Most people have been in a hotel room and been disturbed by a knocking housekeeper. She knocks because she's outside and wants to come in. That's what the audience assumes! So, as a comic, you switch the ending at the last minute to surprise them.

This is called a 'reverse' in comedy and it works all the time. The key is that you don't want to use this same formula repetitively, because the ending will then be expected to be switched and you've given away the surprise. Remember, without surprise, there is no laugh.

Review the jokes on the following pages. Despite being very short, do they have the elements of a story? Do they surprise? What about embarrassment or recognition? Use these as a template to create your own. And, like any good comic, practice, practice, practice!

What do you do when you come across an elephant in the jungle?

Wipe it off and say you're sorry.

What's worse than ants in your pants?

Uncles.

What do you do if your girlfriend starts smoking?

Slow down and possibly use some lubricant.

What's the best thing about fingering a gypsy on her period?

You get your palm red for free.

Three tampons are sitting at a bus stop. What do they say to each other?

Nothing. They're stuck up cunts.

How do you get a Nun pregnant?

Dress her up as an altar boy.

If women drink a glass of red wine, it increases the chance of a stroke.

If she drinks the whole bottle, she might even give it a little suck.

How do you find a blind man on a nude beach?

It's not hard.

Why does a mermaid wear seashells?

Because she outgrew her B-shells!

Two deer walk out of a gay bar...

One says to the other, "Man, I can't believe I blew forty bucks in there!"

What's the difference between an oral and a rectal thermometer?

The taste.

What do you call a man who cries while he masturbates?

A tear jerker.

Had a fight with an erection this morning.

I beat it single handedly.

What's the difference between a prostitute and a drug dealer?

A drug dealer can't wash his crack and sell it again.

What does a leper say after having sex with a prostitute?

"Keep the tip."

What's a 6.9?

Another great thing screwed up by a period.

Why isn't there a pregnant Barbie doll?

Because Ken came in another box.

What do a priest and a Christmas tree have in common?

Both of them have balls for purely decorative purposes.

How does a nice girl know when her mother is on the rag?

Her brother's dick tastes funny.

How do you make a woman moan for hours after sex?

Wipe your dick on her curtains.

What is the difference between a circus and a whorehouse?

The circus has a vast array of cunning stunts!

What do you call a hooker with a runny nose?

Full.

What did the banana say to the vibrator?

Why are you shaking? She's going to eat me!

What do you give an elephant with diarrhea?

Lots of room.

What do Michael Jackson and Santa have in common?

After a night of visiting children, they both have empty sacks.

What's the difference between a hockey player and German girl?

A hockey player will take a shower after three periods.

How can you tell if you're in a gay church?

Only half the congregation is kneeling.

What's the difference between a baby and a trampoline?

You take off your boots before you jump on a trampoline.

How do you make a baby spin around?

Blender.

How do you take it back out?

Nachos.

What do you call a dead baby on a wall?

Art.

What do you call a dead baby floating on the water?

Bob.

What do you call a dead baby on the floor?

Matt.

What's worse than 10 babies in a bag?

One baby in 10 bags.

What do your grandma and your baby have in common?

Both may die during intercourse.

What's the difference?

Your grandma's arsehole won't split in two.

 **MAD COMEDY** hopes you enjoyed this collection of hilarious jokes and learned something of the process to create truly filthy jokes. As always, a five-star review on Amazon is appreciated!

Made in the USA
Monee, IL
25 March 2022